OVERWATCH™
WORLD GUIDE

OVERWATCH™
WORLD GUIDE

BY **TERRA WINTERS**

STORY AND ART BY **BLIZZARD ENTERTAINMENT**

SCHOLASTIC INC.

ISBN 978-1-338-11280-1

10 9 8 7 6 5 4 3 2   17 18 19 20 21

Printed in the U.S.A.   40

First printing 2017

Book design by Two Red Shoes Design

TABLE OF
CONTENTS

THE OVERWATCH LEGACY
WELCOME TO THE FUTURE

Yes, this is Earth. But it's not the Earth you know.

Technology and innovation have made things that were once impossible a reality. Humans live side by side with robots called omnics. Some people even live on the moon.

But no world is without conflict. Years ago, in a time of global crisis, a group of heroes stepped forward to save humanity.

This is the story of Overwatch . . .

THE OVERWATCH LEGACY
RISE OF THE ROBOTS

Before there was Overwatch, there was the Omnica Corporation. This revolutionary company figured out a way to mass-produce robots, which they called omnics. Omnica constructed omniums around the world, massive, automated factories that created robots to fit all sorts of needs and situations. The omniums churned out these omnics by the thousands.

But then the omniums started to break down. It was discovered that Omnica could not deliver on all of its promises, and the automated factories were closed.

So the world was shocked when the omniums woke themselves up! Backed by armies of omnics, they launched a military campaign against all humans.

The Omnic Crisis had begun. No one knew then exactly why the omniums were set on destroying humans, and no country's army could figure out how to shut them down again. The omnics kept attacking and attacking, and they adapted to any strategy used against them.

There was no stopping them. Or was there?

AN ELITE TEAM

It was clear no one country could permanently take down the omniums on its own, so the United Nations recruited a small group of individuals with superior physical abilities, sharp minds, and unique talents. These soldiers became known as Overwatch. The Overwatch agents targeted the omnics in a series of dangerous secret missions. They destroyed the omnics' command and control protocols, ending the Omnic Crisis.

The war was over, but Earth was a real mess. Overwatch stayed in operation as a global peacekeeping force for decades, and grew. It attracted not only soldiers but scientists, explorers, and adventurers of every kind. Overwatch performed heroic rescues. They cleaned up destroyed environments. They made great strides in medical care. They became a symbol of hope to an entire generation.

And then everything changed.

THE OVERWATCH LEGACY
THE FALL . . .
AND RISE AGAIN?

Twenty years after Overwatch saved humanity, scandals hit the organization. A series of high-profile mission failures got people talking. Stories of corruption, abuse of power, and shady dealings by Overwatch's top-secret Blackwatch division turned the public against the global peacekeeping force. So the United Nations shut Overwatch down.

That was several years ago. Time passed, and the world seemed to be doing okay. In many parts of the globe, humans and omnics were living together in peace. The economy was good.

But lately, tensions have been rising between humans and omnics. There are whispers of corporations and governments working together to exploit citizens.

Recent news reports say that former Overwatch agents are resurfacing. Is it possible that they've returned to save the world? And will the world welcome them with open arms—or send them back to the shadows?

Keep reading to get to know the many scientists, adventurers, and oddities who are on the rise.

HEROES: DEFENSE

Even though these heroes are strong in defense, they can be useful in offensive missions too.

You know the saying—you can't have a good offense without a strong defense. The *Overwatch* heroes strong in defense specialize in these major functions:

» They guard locations.

» They create choke points: narrow passages for the opponent to pass through.

» They focus on stopping the opposing team's advance on the battlefield.

Just try getting past one of these defensive powerhouses. It's not easy!

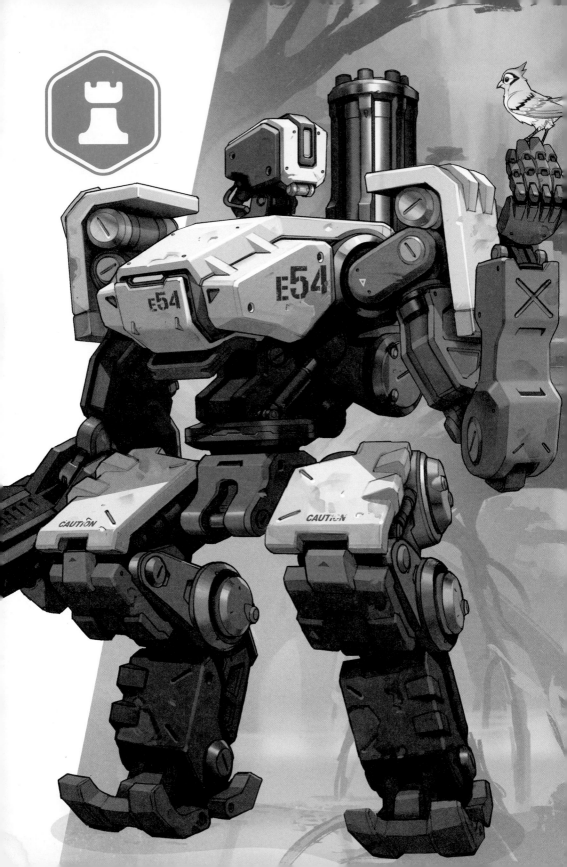

HERO PROFILE:
BASTION

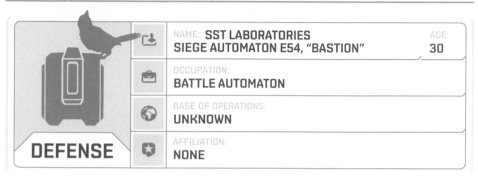

NAME: **SST LABORATORIES SIEGE AUTOMATON E54, "BASTION"**	AGE: **30**
OCCUPATION: **BATTLE AUTOMATON**	
BASE OF OPERATIONS: **UNKNOWN**	

DEFENSE

AFFILIATION: **NONE**

BIOGRAPHY:

Humans originally created Bastion robot units to help keep the peace. Each unit came packed with power—and the ability to quickly transform into an assault cannon! But during the Omnic Crisis, they were turned against the humans and became a major force in the robot army.

After the war, nearly all the Bastion units were destroyed, and those that weren't were left broken down, forgotten for over a decade. While Bastion sat dormant in the wilderness, vines and roots grew over it, and animals nested in it. Then one day, it reactivated.

With its combat programming nearly wiped out, this gentle giant began to wander the Earth, curious about nature and living creatures. It prefers to live in the wild, away from humans. Because when Bastion is threatened, its core programming kicks in, and then, watch out! It will use its abilities to eliminate anything in its path.

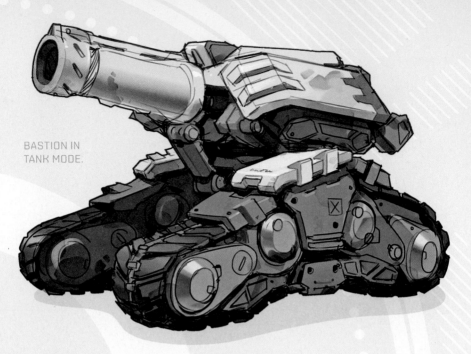

BASTION IN
TANK MODE.

ABILITIES:

ULTIMATE ABILITY— CONFIGURATION: TANK:
Bastion can transform into a tank that delivers major damage with its powerful long-range cannon. But it can't stay in this form for very long.

CONFIGURATION: RECON:
Bastion is fully mobile in this mode and can use its submachine gun to fire steady bursts at medium range.

CONFIGURATION: SENTRY:
When Bastion stands still, it can unleash a hail of bullets with a Gatling gun.

RECONFIGURE:
This ability allows Bastion to quickly switch from Recon mode to Sentry mode during battle.

SELF-REPAIR:
Bastion can restore its own health, but it can't move or fire a weapon while the repair is happening.

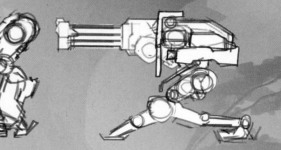

A ROBOT WHO
LIKES BIRDS AND
CHIPMUNKS? IT'S
TRUE. BASTION
HAS A SOFT SPOT
FOR NATURE,
BUT THIS OMNIC
WASN'T ALWAYS
THAT WAY.

HERO PROFILE:
HANZO

NAME:		**AGE:**
HANZO SHIMADA		**38**
OCCUPATION:		
MERCENARY, ASSASSIN		
BASE OF OPERATIONS:		
HANAMURA, JAPAN *(FORMERLY)*		
AFFILIATION:		
SHIMADA CLAN *(FORMERLY)*		

DEFENSE

BIOGRAPHY:

Hanzo is not your ordinary ninja—he can summon the power of a dragon in battle. A former member of the Shimada clan, he was trained in the martial arts and is an expert swordsman and archer. In his darkest moment, Hanzo believed that he had killed his younger brother, Genji. He left the clan and now travels the world as a lone warrior.

ABILITIES:

ULTIMATE ABILITY—DRAGONSTRIKE:
Unleash the dragon! When Hanzo summons his spirit dragon, it can travel through walls to reach his enemies.

STORM BOW:
Hanzo shoots an arrow at his opponent.

SONIC ARROW:
This arrow contains a tracking device to pinpoint enemies.

SCATTER ARROW:
This arrow ricochets off walls and objects to strike many targets at once.

HERO PROFILE:
JUNKRAT

DEFENSE

NAME: **JAMISON FAWKES**		AGE: **25**
OCCUPATION: **ANARCHIST, THIEF, DEMOLITIONIST, MERCENARY, SCAVENGER**		
BASE OF OPERATIONS: **JUNKERTOWN, AUSTRALIA** *[FORMERLY]*		
AFFILIATION: **JUNKERS** *[FORMERLY]*		

BIOGRAPHY:

Junkrat grew up in the Australian Outback. After the war, large parts of the Outback were nearly destroyed, transformed into a wasteland poisoned by radiation from the detonation of the Australian omnium. The people who stayed in the Outback, like Junkrat, survived by scavenging the ruins. Junkrat loves explosives, and even though the radiation has made him a little off-balance, he's a successful thief. He wreaks havoc with his bodyguard, Roadhog.

ABILITIES:

ULTIMATE ABILITY—RIP-TIRE:
This motorized tire bomb can roll over walls and obstacles.

FRAG LAUNCHER:
Grenades shot by the Frag Launcher can bounce to reach their target.

CONCUSSION MINE:
Junkrat can trigger a Concussion Mine to damage enemies and knock them back—or propel himself through the air.

STEEL TRAP:
This giant trap latches on to unsuspecting enemies and doesn't let go.

TOTAL MAYHEM:
If Junkrat gets taken out, he leaves a good-bye present: five grenades.

HERO PROFILE:
MEI

	NAME: **MEI-LING ZHOU**		AGE: **31**
	OCCUPATION: **CLIMATOLOGIST, ADVENTURER**		
	BASE OF OPERATIONS: **XI'AN, CHINA** *(FORMERLY)*		
DEFENSE	AFFILIATION: **OVERWATCH** *(FORMERLY)*		

BIOGRAPHY:

Do you feel that chill? That's Mei, using her weather-changing machine to create a big freeze! After she developed that technology, she was assigned to an Overwatch base in Antarctica. Mei was trained as a climatologist—a scientist who studies weather patterns over time—and she joined a team of scientists studying climate change.

Then a polar storm hit the base, damaging it and leaving the scientists stranded. To survive, they froze themselves in a cryogenics chamber. Overwatch was disbanded, and years later, Mei was rescued—the only scientist to survive the cryostasis, a kind of hibernation.

Mei woke up to a changed world. All of her team's data had been lost. She decided to continue her work on her own. And while Mei knows how to make things frosty, she's got a warm heart. She travels the world with a portable version of her weather-changing technology, hoping to someday save the planet.

ABILITIES:

ULTIMATE ABILITY—BLIZZARD:

Mei can create an instant blizzard with a weather-modification drone that blasts opponents with gusts of wind and snow. It can slow them down—or freeze them solid.

ENDOTHERMIC BLASTER:

This handheld device can shoot streams of frost at close range, or it can shoot out medium-range icicles.

CRYO-FREEZE:

When Mei needs to heal, she can surround herself with a block of thick ice. She can't take any damage in this mode, but she can't move or use abilities, either.

ICE WALL:

This enormous wall of ice can block attacks and hide Mei from her enemies.

MEI CARRIES WEATHER-CHANGING TECHNOLOGY WITH HER WHEREVER SHE GOES.

HERO PROFILE:
TORBJÖRN

	NAME: **TORBJÖRN LINDHOLM**	AGE: **57**
	OCCUPATION: **WEAPONS DESIGNER**	
	BASE OF OPERATIONS: **GOTHENBURG, SWEDEN**	
DEFENSE	AFFILIATION: **OVERWATCH** *(FORMERLY)*	

BIOGRAPHY:

Torbjörn can get fiery when he's angry! But for the most part, this weapons designer has always believed that technology should help humanity, not hurt it. During the Omnic Crisis, he joined Overwatch and developed weapons to overthrow the robots. After Overwatch fell, Torbjörn's weapons were scattered around the world. He constantly searches for them, hoping they won't land in the wrong hands.

ABILITIES:

ULTIMATE ABILITY—MOLTEN CORE:
When Torbjörn overheats his personal forge, it shoots out flames and he glows like molten lava. He also gains armor and scrap, and he can build, repair, and attack faster than normal.

RIVET GUN:
This gun shoots metal rivets or bursts of molten metal.

FORGE HAMMER:
This mighty hammer can build, upgrade, and repair turrets, and it can also be swung as a weapon.

BUILD TURRET:
Torbjörn can build an enemy-tracking autocannon.

ARMOR PACK:
Torbjörn can drop armor upgrades that he or his teammates can pick up to absorb damage.

HERO PROFILE:
WIDOWMAKER

	NAME: **AMÉLIE LACROIX**	AGE: **33**
	OCCUPATION: **ASSASSIN**	
	BASE OF OPERATIONS: **ANNECY, FRANCE**	
DEFENSE	AFFILIATION: **TALON**	

BIOGRAPHY:

Once a normal woman named Amélie, Widowmaker was turned into a cold assassin by the Talon organization. She literally *is* cold—her heart was altered to beat slowly, so her skin always looks blue.

ABILITIES:

ULTIMATE ABILITY—INFRA-SIGHT:
Widowmaker wears a visor that allows her to see the heat signatures of her enemies through walls and objects.

WIDOW'S KISS:
Her sniper rifle has excellent long-distance accuracy, and it can be fired in fully automatic mode at close range.

GRAPPLING HOOK:
This tool allows her to quickly get from one location to another.

VENOM MINE:
This motion-activated mine releases poison gas when triggered.

HEROES: *OFFENSE*

Offense heroes are an asset to any type of mission.

Offense heroes are fast and agile, and they can deliver a lot of damage. Here are some of the things they are best at:

» They can scout ahead of the team and find out what the enemy is up to.

» Because of their ability to move quickly, they can approach enemy teams from behind and get rid of the weakest opponents first.

Heroes with strong offense may often use the element of surprise to startle an enemy. They might swoop down from the skies or appear in the blink of an eye.

HERO PROFILE:
GENJI

NAME: **GENJI SHIMADA**	AGE: **35**
OCCUPATION: **ADVENTURER**	
BASE OF OPERATIONS: **SHAMBALI MONASTERY, NEPAL**	
AFFILIATION: **SHIMADA CLAN** [FORMERLY]**, OVERWATCH** [FORMERLY]	

OFFENSE

BIOGRAPHY:

Part man, part machine, Genji started out as a human; he was the youngest child of the leader of the Shimada clan. When his brother, Hanzo, nearly killed him, Overwatch saved him with omnic technology: cyberization, which gave him faster speed, better agility, and superior ninja skills. Now he has the body of a cyborg but the soul of a human. To find peace with his new form, he became a student of the omnic monk Zenyatta.

ABILITIES:

ULTIMATE ABILITY—DRAGONBLADE:
Genji can use his katana—a long Japanese sword—for short periods. Every blow he strikes with it is a success.

SHURIKEN:
This ninja can hurl three throwing stars quickly in a straight line, or even faster in a wider spread.

DEFLECT:
With lightning-quick swipes of his smaller sword, he can send projectiles shooting back at his opponent.

SWIFT STRIKE:
He can race forward, slashing through foes in his path.

HERO PROFILE:

McCREE

		NAME: **JESSE McCREE**	AGE: **37**
		OCCUPATION: **BOUNTY HUNTER**	
		BASE OF OPERATIONS: **SANTA FE, NEW MEXICO, USA**	
OFFENSE		AFFILIATION: **OVERWATCH** *(FORMERLY)*	

BIOGRAPHY:

This expert marksman has no ties to anyone, but that wasn't always the case. He started out as a smuggler who was recruited by Overwatch for its top-secret division, Blackwatch. Put off by the infighting there, he left Blackwatch and went underground. Now this cowboy is a gunslinger for hire—as long as he believes in your cause.

ABILITIES:

ULTIMATE ABILITY—DEADEYE:
When McCree takes the time to aim, he knows that every one of his shots will hit its target.

PEACEKEEPER:
This cowboy can empty his trusty six-shooter, nicknamed "Peacekeeper," in mere seconds.

COMBAT ROLL:
McCree can dodge danger and load his Peacekeeper at the same time.

FLASHBANG:
This hand grenade can stun several enemies at once.

HERO PROFILE:
PHARAH

	NAME:	AGE:
	FAREEHA AMARI	**32**
	OCCUPATION:	
	SECURITY CHIEF	
	BASE OF OPERATIONS:	
	GIZA, EGYPT	
OFFENSE	AFFILIATION:	
	HELIX SECURITY INTERNATIONAL	

BIOGRAPHY:

When you see Pharah on the battlefield, you'll be in awe of her amazing combat suit. But the suit is only part of her story—underneath the armor beats the heart of a champion.

This soldier began life as a young girl named Fareeha. She dreamed of following in the footsteps of her mother, an Overwatch agent. When Fareeha was old enough, she joined the Egyptian army and quickly worked her way through the ranks. Known for her courageous leadership, Fareeha was a natural for Overwatch—but the organization was disbanded before she could join.

Fareeha went to work for Helix Security International, defending its secret artificial intelligence research facility beneath the desert sands. There, she received training with a mechanical combat suit, the Raptora Mark VI.

Known by the call sign "Pharah," she continues to guard the top-secret facility. But she still dreams of fighting the good fight.

THE RAPTORA MARK VI
SUIT LIGHTS UP WHEN
PHARAH USES BARRAGE.

ABILITIES:

ULTIMATE ABILITY—BARRAGE:
Her combat suit can fire a continuous salvo of
mini-rockets to destroy groups of enemies before
they even know what hit them.

ROCKET LAUNCHER:
Her main weapon can launch rockets that deal major damage in a wide range.

JUMP JET:
Thanks to thrusters in her suit, Pharah can soar high into the air.

CONCUSSIVE BLAST:
Pharah can let loose a wrist rocket that will knock back any opponent it hits.

HERO PROFILE:
REAPER

NAME: **UNKNOWN**		AGE: **N/A**
OCCUPATION: **MERCENARY**		
BASE OF OPERATIONS: **UNKNOWN**		
AFFILIATION: **UNKNOWN**		

OFFENSE

BIOGRAPHY:

Reaper looks like death itself, a disguise calculated to strike fear in the hearts of his opponents. Few know the real identity of this mercenary. But those studying his movements think that he may be hunting down former Overwatch agents and eliminating them, one by one.

ABILITIES:

ULTIMATE ABILITY—DEATH BLOSSOM:
Reaper can empty his twin Hellfire Shotguns before opponents have a chance to react.

HELLFIRE SHOTGUNS:
These shotguns can do serious damage to opponents, especially at close range.

WRAITH FORM:
Reaper can become a shadow for a short period of time and pass through his enemies. He won't take any damage, but he also can't fire his weapons or use his other abilities.

SHADOW STEP:
After marking a destination, Reaper can disappear and reappear in that location.

HERO PROFILE:

SOLDIER: 76

	NAME: **UNKNOWN**		AGE: **N/A**
	OCCUPATION: **VIGILANTE**		
	BASE OF OPERATIONS: **UNKNOWN**		
OFFENSE	AFFILIATION: **OVERWATCH** *(FORMERLY)*		

BIOGRAPHY:

This masked man of mystery got attention by attacking crooked corporations and banks as well as secure Overwatch facilities. The public doesn't know what to make of him. Is he a hero? A criminal? Some claim he is a former Overwatch agent trying to shed light on what really brought down the organization.

Because his physical abilities are superhuman, it is believed that he was trained as part of the American "soldier enhancement program." He supplements his own strength and speed with weapons stolen from Overwatch facilities.

One thing is known for sure about Soldier: 76. He will not stop until he finds those responsible for Overwatch's fall and brings them to justice.

ABILITIES:

ULTIMATE ABILITY—TACTICAL VISOR:
This eye visor can lock on to a target with incredible precision.

HEAVY PULSE RIFLE:
This rifle remains steady while unleashing fully automatic pulse fire.

HELIX ROCKETS:
Tiny rockets spiral out of the Pulse Rifle in a single burst.

SPRINT:
Soldier: 76 has the ability to rush forward at top speed so he can avoid conflicts—or quickly enter them.

BIOTIC FIELD:
This energy emitter will restore the health of Soldier: 76 as well as the health of any of his teammates within the field.

BIOTIC FIELD SPEEDS UP
COMBAT RECOVERY.

TACTICAL VISOR ALLOWS
FOR PRECISE AIMING.

HERO PROFILE:
TRACER

OFFENSE

NAME:		AGE:
LENA OXTON		**26**
OCCUPATION:		
ADVENTURER		
BASE OF OPERATIONS:		
LONDON, ENGLAND		
AFFILIATION:		
OVERWATCH *[FORMERLY]*		

BIOGRAPHY:

A hero who can slow down and speed up her own time? That's Tracer, but she wasn't born that way. Her life changed the day she piloted an Overwatch experimental fighter and the teleportation matrix malfunctioned. The aircraft disappeared, and when Tracer turned up months later, her molecules were out of sync with time. She had become a living ghost, unable to stay in her physical form for more than a few moments.

Overwatch agent Winston found a way to help her. He developed the chronal accelerator, a device that keeps Tracer anchored in the present. But she can use the device to slow down her own time or speed it up, which gives her an advantage in combat situations.

The fall of Overwatch left Tracer with a lot of time on her hands. She spends it righting wrongs and fighting the good fight whenever she can.

> **>>> INCIDENT REPORT <<<**
>
> CALLSIGN:
> **TRACER**
> NAME:
> LENA OXTON
> TIME OF INCIDENT:
> 1107
> CURRENT STATUS:
> MISSING IN ACTION
>
> PROFILE: LEFT
>
> **>>> INCIDENT REPORT <<<**

TRACER OWES HER TIME-TRAVELING ABILITIES TO A FREAK ACCIDENT IN THE SLIPSTREAM, A PROTOTYPE OF A TELEPORTING FIGHTER CRAFT.

ABILITIES:

ULTIMATE ABILITY—PULSE BOMB:

Tracer lobs a bomb that sticks to any target it hits. After a brief delay, the bomb explodes, dealing high damage to any enemies within range.

PULSE PISTOLS:

She wields a rapid-fire pistol in each hand.

BLINK:

In the time it takes to blink, Tracer can disappear and reappear a few yards away—thanks to her ability to speed up her time.

RECALL:

Out of ammo? Injured? No problem for Tracer. She can go backward in her own time and return to where she was a few seconds before—with ammo and health intact.

THE CHRONAL
ACCELERATOR
HELPS KEEP
TRACER ANCHORED
IN THE PRESENT.

HEROES:
SUPPORT

Not every *Overwatch* hero is a warrior. Some of the important members of any fighting team offer support. Here are just some of the things Support heroes might do:

» They can heal team members.

» They can "buff" a team member by giving them a positive upgrade, such as making them faster.

» They can "debuff" an enemy by giving them a negative downgrade, such as making them slower.

» They can build things to help give their team an advantage.

Support heroes might not be the biggest or the baddest, but you wouldn't want to be on a team without one!

HERO PROFILE:
ANA

	NAME:	AGE:
	ANA AMARI	**60**
	OCCUPATION:	
	BOUNTY HUNTER	
	BASE OF OPERATIONS:	
	CAIRO, EGYPT	
SUPPORT	AFFILIATION:	
	OVERWATCH *[FORMERLY]*	

BIOGRAPHY:

Ana Amari was once considered the world's most skilled sniper. She was a natural pick for the Overwatch strike team that ended the Omnic Crisis, and she was later second-in-command. She stayed on active duty well into her fifties, when she was thought to have been killed by Widowmaker. In truth, Ana survived . . . though her right eye didn't. She reconsidered her involvement in the world's conflicts, but as time passed, she could no longer watch from the sidelines. Ana has rejoined the fight.

ABILITIES:

ULTIMATE ABILITY—NANO BOOST:
After Ana hits an ally with a combat boost, they temporarily move faster, deal more damage, and take less damage.

BIOTIC RIFLE:
This rifle can deal damage to her enemies and restore health to her allies.

SLEEP DART:
This dart will knock an enemy unconscious, but further damage will wake that enemy up.

BIOTIC GRENADE:
Allies in this bomb's area of effect receive increased healing, while enemies caught in the blast cannot be healed temporarily.

HERO PROFILE:
LÚCIO

	NAME:	AGE:
	LÚCIO CORREIA DOS SANTOS	**26**
	OCCUPATION:	
	DJ, FREEDOM FIGHTER	
	BASE OF OPERATIONS:	
	RIO DE JANEIRO, BRAZIL	
SUPPORT	AFFILIATION:	
	NONE	

BIOGRAPHY:

Spinning wild beats, long dreads bouncing on his shoulders, Lúcio makes a splash whenever he appears. This musical artist energizes large crowds when he performs, but he's more than just a DJ—he's a hero to the people.

Lúcio grew up in Rio de Janeiro, Brazil, and quickly discovered he had a gift for music. He became legendary for performing in underground shows, and it looked like the party would never end—until the Vishkar Corporation came to Rio.

Vishkar started imposing strict rules on the residents, enforcing curfews and cracking down on what the company called "lawless" behavior. Lúcio fought back. He repurposed Vishkar sonic technology and used it to start a revolution. The residents of Rio de Janeiro drove Vishkar out of their neighborhoods.

Lúcio became an overnight superstar, and he set out on a world tour. "My heart beats for Brazil," he told Atlas News. "I get inspired by the people here. Their struggles. Their triumphs. I want to share that energy—the energy of their lives—with the rest of the world."

THE SONIC AMPLIFIER CAN BE USED OFFENSIVELY OR DEFENSIVELY.

ABILITIES:

ULTIMATE ABILITY—SOUND BARRIER:
When Lúcio activates his Sonic Amplifier, protective waves flow out, providing him and his teammates with temporary personal shields.

SONIC AMPLIFIER:
What's that sound? It's the sound of Lúcio's enemies falling when he hits them with sonic projectiles or powerful sound blasts.

CROSSFADE:
Lúcio and his teammates are constantly charged with energy from his music. He can switch between two songs: one that boosts speed, and another that restores health.

AMP IT UP:
When Lúcio turns up the volume on his songs, it increases their effects.

LÚCIO'S HARD-LIGHT SKATES ALLOW HIM TO MOVE QUICKLY ACROSS ALL SURFACES.

HERO PROFILE:
MERCY

SUPPORT

	NAME: **ANGELA ZIEGLER**	AGE: **37**
	OCCUPATION: **FIELD MEDIC, FIRST RESPONDER**	
	BASE OF OPERATIONS: **ZÜRICH, SWITZERLAND**	
	AFFILIATION: **OVERWATCH** *[FORMERLY]*	

BIOGRAPHY:

You can't make an appointment with this doctor, but if you're hurt, she'll come to your aid in a flash. A brilliant surgeon, Dr. Angela Ziegler was head of medical research for Overwatch. Since the fall of Overwatch, she has traveled the world, aiding innocent victims of war. Wearing the Valkyrie swift-response suit, she can quickly fly to help someone hurt on the battlefield. To many, Mercy is an angel on Earth.

ABILITIES:

ULTIMATE ABILITY—RESURRECT:
Mercy can bring downed allies back to life with full health.

CADUCEUS STAFF:
When a beam from this staff touches one of Mercy's teammates, she can restore their health or increase the damage they deal.

CADUCEUS BLASTER:
Mercy has a sidearm to use for emergency personal defense.

GUARDIAN ANGEL:
Mercy can quickly fly to friends who need help.

ANGELIC DESCENT:
Her Valkyrie suit allows her to fall slowly from great heights.

HERO PROFILE:
SYMMETRA

	NAME:	AGE:
	SATYA VASWANI	28
	OCCUPATION: ARCHITECH	
	BASE OF OPERATIONS: UTOPAEA, INDIA	
SUPPORT	AFFILIATION: VISHKAR CORPORATION	

BIOGRAPHY:

Satya Vaswani is a light-bending architech. Using technology from the Vishkar Corporation, she can instantly transform cities into the clean, orderly places the company desires. She's so good at what she does that Vishkar has dubbed her "Symmetra" and sends her out on undercover missions to uphold Vishkar's interests and spread its influence.

ABILITIES:

ULTIMATE ABILITY—TELEPORTER:
Symmetra can use teleporter exit and entry pads to quickly transport her entire team from one point to another.

PHOTON PROJECTOR:
This weapon shoots out a beam that causes continuous, increasing damage to an enemy once it makes contact. The projector can also release a charged energy ball that deals high damage.

SENTRY TURRET:
Symmetra can set up a turret that automatically fires speed-reducing blasts at nearby enemies.

PHOTON SHIELD:
Symmetra can surround her allies with this damage-absorbing shield.

HERO PROFILE:
ZENYATTA

NAME: **TEKHARTHA ZENYATTA**		AGE: **20**
OCCUPATION: **WANDERING GURU, ADVENTURER**		
BASE OF OPERATIONS: **SHAMBALI MONASTERY, NEPAL** *(FORMERLY)*		
AFFILIATION: **THE SHAMBALI** *(FORMERLY)*		

SUPPORT

BIOGRAPHY:

Do robots have souls? That's the question that a group of outcast robots asked themselves after the Omnic Crisis. They fled to the mountains of the Himalayas and meditated for years. In the end, they agreed that omnic robots possessed souls, just like humans.

These robot monks became world famous and led a movement trying to bring robots and humans together through their teachings. Zenyatta is one robot monk who decided to come down from the mountains to spread this message far and wide.

This robot monk believes the best way to repair the relationship between humans and omnics is for the two species to connect with each other. He travels the world, helping those he meets to find inner peace. And while he himself is peaceful, he will use force to defend himself—and others—when necessary.

ZENYATTA'S ORBS ARE CARVED AT THE MONASTERY TO CHANNEL OMNIC ENERGY. THEY CAN BE USED IN PEACEFUL OR DESTRUCTIVE WAYS.

ABILITIES:

ULTIMATE ABILITY—TRANSCENDENCE:
Zenyatta enters an altered state for a short period of time. While transcendent, he can't use any of his other abilities or weapons. But he can fully restore his own health, along with the health of nearby allies.

ORB OF DESTRUCTION:
When attacked, Zenyatta will fight back. He can project one of these exploding orbs or shoot them repeatedly, rapid-fire.

ORB OF HARMONY:
If one of his allies needs healing, Zenyatta casts this orb over his friend's shoulder to slowly restore them. He can only aid one teammate at a time with this orb.

ORB OF DISCORD:
When this orb attaches to one of Zenyatta's opponents, it will increase the amount of damage that opponent takes.

HEROES: TANK

Tank heroes are massive characters whose purpose is to protect team members by taking damage for them. Here are some Tank hero highlights:

» Their high health pool and strong armor mean they can take damage for longer periods than other characters, and are hard to take down.

» They can jump into a heated battle and disrupt the enemy without being taken out.

» These powerhouses are also great for leading the charge into battle.

They might not be the fastest heroes around, but when you've got a Tank on your team, there's a good chance you'll get the job done!

HERO PROFILE:

D.VA

	NAME:	AGE:
	HANA SONG	**19**
	OCCUPATION:	
	PRO GAMER *(FORMERLY)*, **MECH PILOT**	
	BASE OF OPERATIONS:	
	BUSAN, SOUTH KOREA	
TANK	AFFILIATION:	
	MOBILE EXO-FORCE OF THE KOREAN ARMY	

BIOGRAPHY:

What's more fun than being a professional gamer, getting paid to blast digital robots for a living? How about piloting a giant mech in the military and blasting robots in real life? That's what D.Va does!

D.Va's destiny began years ago, when a colossal omnic rose from the depths of the East China Sea and attacked South Korea. The government responded with a mechanized robot program called MEKA. It recruited professional gamers to pilot the giant mechs.

At the time, Hana Song was the reigning world gaming champion known as D.Va. She was famous for being a fierce competitor who showed no mercy to her opponents—just what was needed to fight the monster omnic in the sea.

These days, D.Va charges fearlessly into battle with the rest of her MEKA unit. She streams combat operations to her adoring fans, who cheer every move this hero makes.

ABILITIES:

ULTIMATE ABILITY—
SELF-DESTRUCT/CALL MECH:

This is a two-part ability. First, D.Va can eject from her mech and set it to explode, causing damage to nearby opponents. Then she can call down a fresh mech and return to the fight.

FUSION CANNONS:

D.Va's mech is equipped with two short-range cannons that can fire continuously without having to reload. When she uses them, they slow down her movement.

BOOSTERS:

D.Va's mech can launch into the air, changing direction or barreling through enemies to knock them back.

DEFENSE MATRIX:

When projectiles are hurtling toward D.Va, she can shoot them out of the air.

LIGHT GUN:

When she's outside her mech, D.Va can still fight, using this midrange automatic blaster.

D.VA'S TWIN FUSION CANNONS DELIVER BIG DAMAGE AT SHORT RANGE.

A MECH FIGHTING SUIT IS LIKE A WALKING TANK.

REINHARDT

📥	NAME: **REINHARDT WILHELM**	AGE: **61**
💼	OCCUPATION: **ADVENTURER**	
🌐	BASE OF OPERATIONS: **STUTTGART, GERMANY**	
⭐	AFFILIATION: **OVERWATCH** [FORMERLY]	

TANK

BIOGRAPHY:

Like a knight in shining armor, Reinhardt fights for justice and to protect the innocent. But his Crusader armor does more than shine—it's enhanced to give him superhuman strength and abilities.

Reinhardt was a German soldier before he joined Overwatch as an agent. After the Omnic Crisis ended, this hero worked hard to keep peace in a war-torn world. He firmly believed that Overwatch could be a force for good. Then, when he reached his late fifties, he was forced to retire.

The sidelined soldier watched as Overwatch was accused of corruption and finally disbanded. Disgusted, Reinhardt couldn't stand by any longer. He has donned his Crusader armor again and has vowed to continue the fight for justice, hoping for better days to come.

THIS MASSIVE ROCKET HAMMER IS SO HEAVY THAT IT NEEDS ROCKETS TO GIVE IT MOMENTUM.

ABILITIES:

ULTIMATE ABILITY—EARTHSHATTER:
Reinhardt forcefully slams his hammer into the ground, knocking down and damaging all the enemies in front of him.

ROCKET HAMMER:
This weapon deals punishing damage in a wide arc with every swing.

BARRIER FIELD:
When Reinhardt projects this energy barrier in front of him, he can't attack. But he can protect himself and his companions from substantial damage while it is up.

CHARGE:
When Reinhardt charges forward with rocket power, he can grab an enemy and then slam into a wall. Reinhardt's armor will protect him, but his foe will take extreme damage.

FIRE STRIKE:
Reinhardt's hammer can sling a flaming projectile that will damage any enemy it touches.

HERO PROFILE:
ROADHOG

	NAME: **MAKO RUTLEDGE**		AGE: **48**
	OCCUPATION: **ENFORCER** *(FORMERLY)*, **BODYGUARD**		
	BASE OF OPERATIONS: **JUNKERTOWN, AUSTRALIA** *(FORMERLY)*		
TANK	AFFILIATION: **JUNKERS** *(FORMERLY)*		

BIOGRAPHY:

Roadhog is more beast than man, but he wasn't always this way. He started life as Mako Rutledge, a guy living in the Australian Outback. When the government gave Outback land to omnics after the Omnic Crisis, Mako and others rebelled. The violent battle left the Outback a radioactive wasteland. That's why Roadhog wears a mask. You can usually find him hanging out with his friend Junkrat.

ABILITIES:

ULTIMATE ABILITY—WHOLE HOG:
Roadhog can crank out a stream of shrapnel from his Scrap Gun.

SCRAP GUN:
This weapon can repurpose any scrap metal into ammunition.

TAKE A BREATHER:
When he's hurt, he can restore a chunk of his health.

CHAIN HOOK:
Opponents caught by Roadhog's chain get yanked into close range—which is not a good place to be!

HERO PROFILE:
WINSTON

	NAME: **WINSTON**	AGE: **29**
	OCCUPATION: **SCIENTIST, ADVENTURER**	
	BASE OF OPERATIONS: **WATCHPOINT: GIBRALTAR**	
TANK	AFFILIATION: **OVERWATCH** [FORMERLY]	

BIOGRAPHY:

Winston may look like a big, powerful gorilla, but he is more human—and has a bigger heart—than some of the world's other heroes.

This gorilla's first memories are of life on a moon base, the Horizon Lunar Colony. He and other genetically enhanced gorillas were there to test the effects of living on the moon for a long time. But he developed much more quickly than the others, and he was taken under the wing of Dr. Harold Winston, who taught him science.

Tragedy struck when the other gorillas rebelled, killing all the humans on the moon. This gorilla took the name Winston after his beloved human caretaker, and then he built a rocket ship, fled to Earth, and became an Overwatch agent.

Even when Overwatch fell, Winston never lost faith in humanity. There is no place in this world for him now, and he lives in seclusion. But when Winston is called in to fight for what's right—watch out! He is massively strong and will destroy anything in his path when his animal nature takes over.

ABILITIES:

ULTIMATE ABILITY—PRIMAL RAGE:
When Winston embraces his animal nature, he becomes an almost unstoppable force. This ability boosts his health, strengthens his melee attack, and allows him to use his Jump Pack ability more frequently. While raging, he can't use any other abilities except for melee and Jump Pack—but he is nearly impossible to take down.

TESLA CANNON:
This weapon fires a continuous barrage of electric energy at short range.

JUMP PACK:
Winston's energy pack allows him to lunge through the air, dealing significant damage to anything he makes contact with.

BARRIER PROJECTOR:
This device projects a bubble-shaped field that protects Winston and his allies from damage until it's destroyed. Allies protected by the barrier can return fire from within it.

YOUNG WINSTON

WHEN WINSTON
USES PRIMAL RAGE,
WATCH OUT!

HERO PROFILE:
ZARYA

	📥	NAME: **ALEKSANDRA ZARYANOVA**	AGE: **28**
	💼	OCCUPATION: **SOLDIER**	
	🌐	BASE OF OPERATIONS: **KRASNOYARSK FRONT, RUSSIA**	
TANK	🛡	AFFILIATION: **RUSSIAN DEFENSE FORCES**	

BIOGRAPHY:

Need some muscle for your team? Someone who will do anything to protect her friends and family? Then call on Zarya.

When she was a little girl in Siberia, Zarya saw her village devastated by the war against the omnics. Her people defeated the robots and their omnium—a massive robot-producing factory—but at a high cost. Seeing the destruction around her, Zarya vowed that she would gain the strength to help her people recover.

She grew up to be a champion weightlifter and bodybuilder. But before she could enter the world championships, the omnium became active again and her village was attacked. She quickly returned home and joined the local defense forces, sacrificing fame and fortune to help her people.

Zarya's massive build allows her to wield mighty weapons and fight off attackers. But her true strength comes from the love and loyalty she has for those she cares about.

ZARYA RIPPED HER PARTICLE CANNON FROM THE HULL OF AN ARMORED VEHICLE. IT'S FAR TOO HEAVY FOR MOST SOLDIERS TO CARRY, BUT FOR ZARYA, IT'S NO PROBLEM.

ZARYA CAN STILL FIRE HER WEAPON WHEN SHE'S PROTECTED BY THE PARTICLE BARRIER.

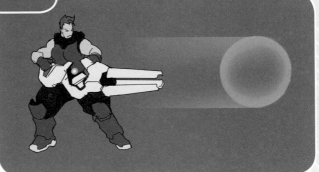

ABILITIES:

ULTIMATE ABILITY—GRAVITON SURGE:
Zarya launches a gravity bomb that draws her enemies toward it. While they're trapped, they are dealt serious damage.

PARTICLE CANNON:
Bring on the boom! Zarya's Particle Cannon can unleash a short-range beam of destructive energy or produce a blast to strike multiple opponents.

PARTICLE BARRIER:
The Particle Cannon can emit a protective shield for Zarya. Not only does it prevent her from receiving damage, but it redirects the energy to widen the beam of the Particle Cannon and increase the damage it can dish out.

PROJECTED BARRIER:
Zarya can give one of her teammates a protective shield, which will also boost the power of her Particle Cannon.

ENVIRONMENTS

What is the world like in the wake of the Omnic Crisis? It looks a lot like the world you know, but enhanced with technology. And wherever you go, the threat of danger is always present.

ENVIRONMENT:
DORADO

E	**OBJECTIVE DETAILS:** ESCORT
	COUNTRY: MEXICO
	FLAG: 

A NEW ERA DAWNS

When the Omnic Crisis ended, the colorful city of Dorado, Mexico, was plunged into darkness, thanks to a destroyed power grid. Each year, residents celebrate this event with the Festival de la Luz. But a new day is about to dawn in Dorado, with the opening of fusion plants providing clean, free energy to the Mexican people.

ENVIRONMENT:
HANAMURA

A	OBJECTIVE DETAILS: **ASSAULT**
	COUNTRY: **JAPAN**
	FLAG: 🔴

NINJA SECRETS

The trees in this peaceful Japanese village burst into bloom every spring, blanketing the town in pink blossoms. But Hanamura has a dangerous past. It was once home to the powerful Shimada family, a ninja clan that transformed into a criminal organization. Now there is danger lurking inside the former Shimada compound, hidden in the shadows . . .

ENVIRONMENT:
HOLLYWOOD

AE	OBJECTIVE DETAILS: **ASSAULT/ESCORT**
	COUNTRY: **USA**
	FLAG:

TROUBLE IN TINSELTOWN

Hollywood survived the Omnic Crisis with all its glitz and glamour intact. Palm trees line the streets. Movie stars, directors, and high-powered studio executives work here. These days, one of the popular directors is a robot: HAL-Fred Glitchbot, creator of *They Came from Beyond the Moon* and *Six-Gun Killer*. But while Glitchbot has his fans, he has been targeted by the anti-omnic movement thanks to his outspoken opinions. Will this robot's real-life story end in tragedy or triumph?

ENVIRONMENT:
ILIOS

OBJECTIVE DETAILS:
CONTROL

COUNTRY:
GREECE

FLAG:

WELCOME TO PARADISE

This vacation destination is located atop a small island in the Aegean Sea. It features bustling shops, winding paths, and gorgeous views. Some people come here to rest and relax, while others choose to explore the ruins scattered at the top of the island. Many ancient relics have recently been unearthed there.

ENVIRONMENT:
KING'S ROW

OBJECTIVE DETAILS:
ASSAULT/ESCORT

COUNTRY:
UNITED KINGDOM

FLAG:

THE CITY BENEATH THE CITY

King's Row is a busy, thriving neighborhood in London—thanks to the labor of omnic robots. Those robot workers have been denied basic rights and are forced to live in a crowded city underneath the streets of London known as "the Underworld." Some humans support the omnics, but protesters recently clashed violently with police during a pro-omnic demonstration. Tensions are running high—like a powder keg about to explode on King's Row.

ENVIRONMENT:

LIJIANG TOWER

	OBJECTIVE DETAILS:
C	**CONTROL**
	COUNTRY:
	CHINA
	FLAG:

SIGHTS ON SPACE

This tall, majestic tower rises up from the streets of a busy city in China, overlooking shops, gardens, and restaurants. The tower itself is owned by a company that is pushing the boundaries of space exploration. But what, exactly, does Lucheng Interstellar hope to find in the deep regions of the universe?

ENVIRONMENT:
NEPAL

OBJECTIVE DETAILS:
CONTROL

COUNTRY:
NEPAL

FLAG:

WHERE SEEKERS GATHER

The country of Nepal has long been a destination for people seeking enlightenment. So years ago, when a group of omnics had a spiritual awakening, they came here and founded Shambali Monastery. They were led by Tekhartha Mondatta before his death. He taught them how to meditate on the meaning of existence. Both humans and omnics are welcome to study with the robot monks.

ENVIRONMENT:
NUMBANI

	**OBJECTIVE DETAILS:** **ASSAULT/ESCORT** **CONTINENT:** **AFRICA** **FLAG:**

CITY OF HARMONY

This African city is one of the few places in which humans and omnics can live as equals. When humans and omnics work together, amazing technology is created. Each year, this partnership between robots and humans is celebrated on Unity Day. But will the festivities be threatened by those who oppose what the City of Harmony represents?

ENVIRONMENT:
ROUTE 66

E	**OBJECTIVE DETAILS:** **ESCORT**
	COUNTRY: **USA**
	FLAG:

HOME TO OUTLAWS

This highway was once America's most popular road, lined with gleaming diners and roadside attractions. Today, most of the gas stations, shops, and restaurants are empty. A cross-country train runs along the route, and passengers stare out the windows at ghost towns, like Deadlock Gorge, as they pass by. But Deadlock Gorge isn't totally deserted—it is home to the notorious Deadlock Gang, and they're about to make their biggest heist yet.

ENVIRONMENT:

TEMPLE OF ANUBIS

OBJECTIVE DETAILS:
ASSAULT

COUNTRY:
EGYPT

FLAG:

MYSTERY IN THE DESERT

You may have heard of the Giza Plateau in Egypt, home to many great pyramids. After the Omnic Crisis, explorers unearthed a new discovery in the desert sands: the Temple of Anubis. Many don't know that this is more than just a tourist attraction. It hides the entrance to a research facility that extends deep beneath the earth. Only a few agents at Helix Security International, the private firm that guards the facility, know what they're protecting.

ENVIRONMENT:

VOLSKAYA INDUSTRIES

OBJECTIVE DETAILS:
ASSAULT

COUNTRY:
RUSSIA

FLAG:

WHERE MECHS ARE BORN

After Russia was nearly destroyed by the Omnic Crisis, it took years for the country to recover. And it did, becoming a center of cutting-edge technology. So when the Siberian omnium became active again, churning out battle-ready omnics, the Russians were prepared. Volskaya Industries produces Svyatogor mechs—huge robots piloted by humans—capable of confronting new omnic threats head-on.

ENVIRONMENT:

WATCHPOINT: GIBRALTAR

OBJECTIVE DETAILS:
ESCORT

TERRITORY:
GIBRALTAR

FLAG:

EYES TO THE SKIES

When Overwatch was at its height, it established several bases around the world. Watchpoint: Gibraltar was set up as an orbital launch facility, a spaceport designed to send spacecraft into orbit. Overwatch veteran Winston has taken refuge here. Sensing that the world needed help, he began recalling former Overwatch agents and putting them back into action.

WHAT KIND OF HERO WILL YOU BE?

By now your mind is probably spinning with questions. Can humans and omnics really live in peace? Is Overwatch dangerous, or is it the only thing that can save the world?

There's only one way to figure out where you stand. Suit up. Gear up. Jump into the battle.

Then find out what kind of hero you are . . .